LTL

ALLEN COUNTY PUBLIC LIBRARY

3 1833 03803 3913

D1240762

BEST BIBLE STORIES

The Man Who Was Not Tall Enough

THE MAN WHO WAS NOT TALL ENOUGH

Jennifer Rees Larcombe

Illustrated by Steve Björkman

CROSSWAY BOOKS • WHEATON, ILLINOIS
A DIVISION OF GOOD NEWS PUBLISHERS

The Man Who Was Not Tall Enough
Text copyright © 1992, 1997 by Jennifer Rees Larcombe
Illustrations copyright © 1997 by Steve Björkman
U. S. edition published 1999 by Crossway Books
a division of Good News Publishers
1300 Crescent Street
Wheaton, Illinois 60187
First British edition published 1992
by Marshall Pickering as part of *Children's Bible Story Book.*
This book published as a separate edition in 1997
by Marshall Pickering, an Imprint of HarperCollins Religious,
part of HarperCollins Publishers,
77-85 Fulham Palace Road, London W6 8JB.
All rights reserved. No part of this publication may be reproduced,
stored in a retrieval system, or transmitted in any form by any means,
electronic, mechanical, photocopy, recording, or otherwise,
without the prior permission of the publisher, except as provided by
USA copyright law.
Cover design: Cindy Kiple
First U. S. printing 1999
Printed in Hong Kong
ISBN 1-58134-052-4

THE MAN WHO WAS
NOT TALL ENOUGH

LUKE 19:1–10

Nobody in Jericho liked Zacchaeus.

"He's a greedy little liar," they all said.

"Imagine working for the Romans!

He tells us they want even more of our money than they really do, so he can keep some for himself.

He's made himself rich with OUR money!"

People

never

spoke

to him

in the

street,

and every night he sat alone in his grand house eating food fit for a party,

but no one ever came to share it. Zacchaeus pretended he did not care, but inside he was desperately lonely.

One day, as he worked in his office, he heard a great buzz of excitement outside in the street.

"He's coming past on his way up to Jerusalem," everyone was saying. "Who's coming?" Zacchaeus asked one of his servants.

"Jesus of Nazareth," he told him.

Zaccheus began to tremble. For three years now he had been hearing stories about this man. The piles of

gold coins on his desk suddenly

seemed **unimportant.**

He knew he just wanted to see Jesus. His servants were astounded when he jumped up and dashed out into the street. "I'll have to get to the front of this crowd," he thought. "I'm so **short** I can't see over their heads."

"Go away, Zacchaeus," everyone said as he tried to squeeze past them, and they prodded him back with their elbows. "We don't want Jesus to see you; you're a disgrace to the town."

"I'll run on ahead," he thought desperately, "and climb that old sycamore tree I used to play in when I was a boy. If I hide among the leaves, I can look down and see everything, but no one will see me."

The sight of a fat, little man struggling up a tree would have **made everyone laugh,** but no one saw Zacchaeus; they were too busy watching for Jesus.

It was easy
to guess
which man was Jesus
and, as he clung nervously
to the branches,
Zacchaeus thought he had
never seen anyone with such a

kind face before. It made him

remember all the bad things he had done and he

wished to start all over again.

The next minute he nearly fell out of the tree with surprise. Jesus stopped and looked straight up at him through the leaves.

"Zaccheus, come down.

I'm on my way to

stay
with
you."

"He knows who I am, and he STILL wants to come to my house!" gasped Zacchaeus.

The good people of Jericho were jealous. "We're the kind of people Jesus should visit," they sniffed, "not nasty men like that."

"It was for **bad** people that I came," said Jesus,

"so that I could save them from their sins."

What a party they had.

Zacchaeus could not remember ever being so happy.

"I am going to give half my money to the poor," he told everyone. "And after that I will pay back **four times** as much to everyone who I have cheated."

"Today," smiled Jesus, "God has saved you."

Let's talk about the story

1. Why didn't anyone in Jericho like Zacchaeus?

2. How did that make Zacchaeus feel?

3. Why did Zacchaeus want to see Jesus?

4. Why did Jesus choose to go to Zacchaeus' house and not the house of someone else?

5. If Jesus came to your house how would you feel?

6. Do you know somebody that others don't like or who needs to know that Jesus came to save them? What can you do to help them?